Laid Off at 40+: Your 90-Day Comeback Plan

From Crisis to Comeback — The Urgent Action Plan After Job Loss

Niramaya Iyer

ISBN: 978-93-47365-24-9

First Edition

Title: Laid Off at 40+: Your 90-Day Comeback Plan
Subtitle: From Crisis to Comeback: The Urgent Action Plan After Job Loss
Author: Niramaya Iyer

Published by:
Divamani Enterprises
Ernakulam, India
Website: www.divamani.in
Email: divamani.enterprises@divamani.in

Contents

When the Ground Shifts

Ramesh, 47, senior manager, fifteen years with the company. The conference room invitation appeared on his calendar at 9:47 AM — "Quick sync with HR." He knew immediately. You always know.

Thirty minutes later, he walked out carrying a cardboard box and a severance letter. Two kids in college. Home loan EMI of ₹45,000 every month. Parents' medical expenses. The floor had disappeared beneath his feet.

If this sounds familiar, you're not alone. The layoffs of 2023-2025 hit everyone — Google, Microsoft, Meta, Amazon, and dozens of Indian startups. AI is accelerating the disruption. And if you're over 40, you already know the truth: age makes you expensive and "not a culture fit" in hiring manager speak.

No one is truly safe anymore.

This book is for you if:

- You were laid off in the last 30 days and you're in crisis mode
- You're facing an imminent layoff and need to prepare now
- You feel vulnerable in your current role and want prevention strategies

What you'll achieve in 90 days:

Days 1-30: Emergency stabilization. You'll secure your cash flow, negotiate your severance, cut costs strategically, and generate immediate income. No panic moves – just systematic crisis management.

Days 31-60: Strategic assessment. You'll audit your seven distinct assets, reframe your experience as advantage, and position yourself for the market that exists today, not the one you wish existed.

Days 61-90: Multiple income launch. You'll build 1-2 income streams so you never depend entirely on one job again. This isn't about getting back to where you were – it's about building something more resilient.

How to use this book:

Red zone (less than 3 months runway): Read Parts 1-2 immediately. Implement today, not tomorrow.

Yellow zone (3-6 months): Read Part 1, then work through Parts 2-3 methodically.

Green zone (6+ months): Read the full book with a strategic, not panicked, approach.

You will get through this. Here's how.

Part One: Immediate Stabilization (Days 1-30)

Chapter 1: The 72-Hour Emergency Audit

By Hour 72, you'll know exactly where you stand and have a clear action plan.

Sunita, 44, got laid off on a Friday afternoon. She spent the weekend in shock, staring at her phone, alternating between anger and numbness. Monday morning, she finally opened her banking app. Savings account: ₹2.8 lakh. Home loan EMI: ₹45,000. Other monthly expenses: ₹55,000. Simple math: less than three months before she hits zero.

The clock was ticking. She'd already lost 72 hours.

Don't be Sunita.

Hour 1-4: The Shock is Real (and Normal)

First, acknowledge what you're feeling. Fear. Anger. Shame. Panic. Maybe all four at once.

This is normal. You just lost not only your income, but your identity, your routine, your certainty about the future. Let yourself feel it for one hour. Actually feel it – don't push it away.

Then it's time for action mode. Emotions will come in waves over the coming weeks, but right now, you need clarity more than comfort.

Hour 5-8: Liquid Assets Audit

Get out a notebook or open a spreadsheet. List everything you can access immediately:

- **Bank accounts:** Savings, current, anything liquid
- **Fixed deposits:** You can break these if necessary (penalty is cheaper than crisis)
- **Liquid mutual funds:** Can be redeemed in 1-3 days
- **Emergency fund:** This is THE emergency it was meant for
- **Credit available:** Credit cards are last resort, but know what you have

Add it all up. **This number is your runway ammunition.**

Example:

- Savings: ₹2,80,000
- FD: ₹1,50,000 (breakable)
- Emergency fund: ₹1,00,000
- **Total: ₹5,30,000**

Hour 9-16: Obligations Audit

Now list every monthly obligation. Be brutally honest.

Non-negotiable:

- Home loan/rent EMI: ₹45,000
- School fees: ₹12,000
- Insurance premiums: ₹5,000
- Essential utilities: ₹5,000

Negotiable:

- Credit card payments: ₹15,000 (can negotiate payment plans)
- Personal loans: ₹8,000
- Subscriptions: ₹2,000

Cuttable:

- Dining out: ₹8,000
- Entertainment: ₹5,000
- Shopping: ₹10,000

Add up the non-negotiable and negotiable items. **This is your monthly burn rate.**

Example: ₹45K + ₹12K + ₹5K + ₹5K + ₹15K + ₹8K = ₹90,000/ month minimum

Hour 17-24: Calculate Your Fortress Index

Here's your most important number right now:

Fortress Index = Liquid assets ÷ Monthly burn rate = Months of runway

Using our example: ₹5,30,000 ÷ ₹90,000 = 5.9 months

Red zone: Less than 3 months = Emergency measures NOW

Yellow zone: 3-6 months = Aggressive action required

Green zone: 6+ months = Strategic approach, not panic

This number determines your urgency level. Everything you do in the next 90 days depends on this calculation.

If you're in the red zone, you have no time to be picky. If you're in the green zone, you have breathing room to be strategic. Know which one you're in.

Hour 25-48: Severance & Settlement

Contact HR today. Not next week — today.

Understand your separation package:

- Notice period payment (are you actually getting it?)
- Severance package (typically 1-3 months salary — but it's often negotiable)
- Gratuity (if you have 5+ years of service)
- Unused leave encashment
- Extended health insurance (many companies will negotiate this if you ask)

Negotiation tips:

Most people accept the first offer. Don't. Here's what to ask for:

"I appreciate the package. Given my 15 years of service, is there flexibility to extend the severance from 2 months to 4 months?"

"Would it be possible to extend health insurance coverage for 6 months while I'm in transition?"

"Can I get a positive reference letter in writing?"

You'd be surprised how often the answer is yes — if you ask. Companies have more flexibility than they initially reveal, and most HR departments would rather negotiate than deal with conflict.

Get everything in writing. Everything.

Hour 49-72: Emergency Communication Plan

Who to tell, when:

Now:

- Immediate family (spouse, parents if dependent on you)
- One or two close friends for emotional support

Later (when you're ready):

- Extended family
- Professional network on LinkedIn

Not yet:

- Don't blast "I need a job" on LinkedIn on Day 1. You smell desperate, and desperation repels opportunities.

What to say:

To family: "I've been laid off. I've done the math. We have [X] months of runway. Here's the plan: [brief overview]. We'll get through this together."

To your network (when you're ready): "After 15 years at [Company], I'm exploring new opportunities in [domain]. Open to [consulting/full-time/advisory roles]."

What NOT to say:

Don't badmouth your former company. It hurts you, not them. Hiring managers see it as a red flag.

Don't say "I desperately need a job RIGHT NOW." Desperation is the fastest way to get lowball offers.

Don't hide completely. Isolation makes everything worse.

Hour 72: The First Emergency Meeting

If you have family who depends on your income, it's time for the family meeting.

Sit down with your spouse. If your children are old enough to understand (teenagers+), include them at an appropriate level.

Share the numbers: "We have X months of runway. Here's what that means. Here's the plan."

If your spouse is working, their income just became critical. Protect it.

If they're not working, discuss how they can help — emotional support, taking on tasks you used to handle, helping with immediate income generation if possible.

Create a united front. This crisis is managed together, not alone.

Case Studies

Vikram's mistake: Panicked on Day 2. Withdrew ₹5 lakh from his EPF, paid 30% penalty plus tax. Six months later, he got a job and regretted depleting that fund forever.

Anjali's negotiation: Her initial severance offer was 2 months. She asked for 4 months plus extended health insurance. She got it. That extra ₹3 lakh made all the difference.

Prakash's runway: Eight months of savings. He breathed, made better decisions, took time to find the right role. Not desperate = better negotiating position.

Action Steps

- Complete your 72-hour audit today
- Calculate your Fortress Index and write it down: ___ months
- Contact HR if you haven't already
- Have "the conversation" with your family
- Create an emergency spreadsheet to track everything

Key Takeaways

- The first 72 hours determine the next 90 days
- Your Fortress Index is your most important number right now
- Severance is negotiable – most people don't ask, but you should
- Awareness before action; panic makes everything worse

Chapter 2: Strategic Cost Cutting (Not Panic Cutting)

By the end of this chapter, you'll cut ₹15,000-30,000 per month without destroying family morale.

Deepak, 49, panicked the day after his layoff. He cancelled everything: kids' music classes, wife's gym membership, parents' weekly visits, every subscription. He thought he was being responsible.

Six months later: kids resentful, wife depressed, family falling apart. Deepak is still unemployed, but now he's also isolated. The money he saved wasn't worth the cost to family unity.

Don't be Deepak.

The Strategic vs. Panic Framework

Panic cutting destroys morale: - Cut everything indiscriminately - Impose decisions unilaterally on family - Eliminate all joy and normalcy - Result: Miserable family, broken support system when you need it most

Strategic cutting preserves morale: - Cut ruthlessly in luxury areas - Preserve carefully in infrastructure areas - Involve family in decisions - Result: Lower burn rate AND a united family supporting you

Which approach do you want?

The Three-Tier Expense Framework

TIER 1: Cut Immediately (Luxury)

These are wants, not needs. Cut them now:

- **Dining out/ordering in:** ₹8-15K/month saved (cook at home)
- **New clothing:** ₹3-5K/month saved (wear what you own)
- **Gym membership:** ₹2-3K/month saved (switch to home workouts or park runs)
- **Weekend entertainment:** ₹3-5K/month saved (movies at home, not theaters)
- **Cab rides:** ₹3-5K/month saved (metro, bus, or carpool)
- **Premium subscriptions:** ₹2-3K/month saved (cut Netflix Premium to Basic, pause others)

Total Tier 1 cuts: ₹20,000-35,000/month

Yes, this hurts. But these are pure luxuries that you can restore later.

TIER 2: Negotiate (Renegotiable)

These you don't cut — you negotiate:

Home loan EMI: Call your bank and request a moratorium. Post-COVID, most banks offer 3-6 month EMI holidays. Interest still accrues, but your immediate cash flow gets ₹30-50K/month of breathing room. This is your secret weapon.

Credit card payments: Call the bank. Explain the situation. Request a payment plan. Many banks will work with you rather than risk default.

Rent: If you're renting, have an honest conversation with your landlord. "I've been laid off. I can pay, but I need a

10-15% reduction for the next 6 months." Many will negotiate rather than risk vacancy.

Insurance premiums: Don't cancel, but request payment deferral. Cancelling is dangerous; deferring is smart.

School fees: Many schools have hardship policies. Speak to the principal or administration. You'd be surprised.

Total Tier 2 savings: ₹5-10K/month + EMI relief

TIER 3: Preserve (Infrastructure)

Never cut these. Ever.

- **Health insurance:** Medical emergency during unemployment = bankruptcy. Protect this.
- **Children's core education:** School itself, not extras. Tuition can pause; school cannot.
- **Internet:** Essential for job search, consulting, remote work
- **Phone:** Your communication lifeline
- **Nutritious food:** Health = ability to work. Don't compromise here.
- **One family activity:** One movie at home per month. Sunday walks in the park. Something to preserve sanity.

You're cutting expenses, not destroying your family's foundation.

The Family Meeting

Don't impose cuts on your family. Involve them.

Call a family meeting. Explain the situation in age-appropriate terms. For younger kids: "We need to be more careful with money for a while." For teenagers: Be more direct about the numbers.

Ask: "What can we cut together?"

When your 15-year-old suggests cutting their own music classes, you'll know you have a united family. When your spouse suggests their own sacrifices, you'll feel less alone.

Shared sacrifice builds unity. Imposed sacrifice builds resentment.

Monthly Burn Rate Target

Here's a realistic example:

Before layoff: ₹100,000/month

After strategic cuts: ₹60,000-65,000/month

Impact on runway: - Before: 5 months - After: 8+ months

That 3-month extension makes the difference between desperate decisions and strategic choices.

Case Studies

Meera's balance: Cut ₹18K in pure luxury spending (dining, entertainment, shopping). Kept ₹8K for sanity spending (occasional treats, small family activities). Family stayed united through 7-month job search.

Rajiv's EMI moratorium: Negotiated a 6-month home loan holiday. Freed up ₹35K/month in immediate cash flow. Gave him breathing room to find the right role, not the desperate role.

Kavita's false economy: Cancelled kids' internet to save ₹800/month. Kids couldn't do online homework. Family peace destroyed. Not worth it.

Action Steps

- List ALL your expenses from the last 3 months
- Categorize each: Tier 1 (cut) / Tier 2 (negotiate) / Tier 3 (preserve)
- Cut all Tier 1 items this week
- Make negotiation calls for Tier 2 items (bank, landlord, school)
- Hold a family meeting to discuss and decide together
- Calculate your new monthly burn rate
- Recalculate your Fortress Index with the new number

Key Takeaways

- Strategic cuts preserve morale while extending runway — both are critical
- EMI moratorium is your secret weapon — use it
- Involving family creates support; imposing creates resentment
- The goal is runway extension, not misery

Chapter 3: Immediate Cash Flow (Week 1-4)

By Week 4, you'll have generated your first ₹10,000-30,000 from immediate income sources.

Amit, 51, spent eight hours a day on job portals for three months straight. Applied to 200+ positions. Got zero interviews. His savings were almost gone.

His mistake? He never thought about immediate income. He was waiting for the perfect corporate job to appear while his runway burned away.

Don't be Amit.

The Strategic Error of "Job Search Only"

The average job search for someone over 40 takes 4-8 months. That's longer than it took in your 20s or 30s. Age bias is real, competition is fierce, and companies move slowly.

If your runway is 5 months and your job search will take 6-7 months, the math doesn't work.

Better approach: Immediate cash flow + job search in parallel.

The Three Income Tiers

TIER 1: Immediate Cash (Week 1-2)

Target: ₹10,000-30,000 one-time

Sell unused assets:

- Second vehicle (if you have one): ₹50K-2L
- Unused electronics (old laptop, phone, camera): ₹5-20K

- Books, furniture, appliances on OLX: ₹3-10K
- Jewelry (last resort, but it's an option): Variable

Target: ₹20-50K one-time. This extends your runway by 2-4 weeks. Every week matters.

Use credit strategically:

- Emergency fund (this is the emergency)
- Break FD if needed (penalty < crisis)
- Credit card only for essentials (track carefully)
- Personal loan only as absolute last resort (high interest)

TIER 2: Bridge Income (Week 2-4)

Target: ₹15,000-40,000/month

Your 20-year career has skills. They're monetizable right now.

If you're in tech/IT:

- Freelance coding on Upwork, Toptal, Freelancer.in
- Website fixes for small businesses
- Data entry or analysis projects
- Potential: ₹20-40K/month for 40-50 hours of work

If you're in finance/accounting:

- Tax filing for individuals (especially seasonal)
- Bookkeeping for small businesses
- GST return filing
- Potential: ₹15-30K/month for 30-40 hours

If you're in marketing:

- Social media management for SMEs

- Content writing (blogs, website copy, LinkedIn posts)
- Basic SEO consultation
- Potential: ₹15-25K/month for 30-40 hours

If you're in operations/supply chain:

- Process consulting for small manufacturers
- Inventory management setup
- Vendor negotiation projects
- Potential: ₹20-35K/month for 20-30 hours

If you're in HR:

- Recruitment for startups (per-placement fee)
- HR policy documentation for growing companies
- Employee handbook creation
- Potential: ₹15-30K/month for 20-30 hours

If none of the above apply:

- Teaching/tutoring (school subjects, competitive exams): ₹15-25K/month
- Driving (Uber, Ola): ₹25-35K/month (swallow the pride)
- Delivery (Swiggy, Zomato part-time): ₹15-20K/month
- Administrative work in gated communities: ₹15-25K/month

TIER 3: Network Activation (Week 3-4)

Target: Consulting projects worth ₹50K-2L

Former colleagues who've moved to senior positions at other companies might need exactly your expertise. Make a list of 20 people:

- Former team members now at competitors

- Vendors or partners you worked with
- Industry contacts from conferences, associations
- College alumni in your industry

The outreach script:

DON'T say: "I need a job."

DO say: "I'm now available for consulting in [specific area – process optimization, financial modeling, whatever your expertise is]. If you know anyone who could use that expertise, I'd appreciate the introduction."

Reach out to 20 people. Expect 2-3 responses and 1 real opportunity. One project could be ₹50K-2L.

The "Any Ethical Rupee" Principle

Pride is expensive.

₹20,000/month in bridge income = 1-2 months more runway.

1-2 months more runway = better job decisions instead of desperate ones.

No ethical work is beneath you when you're feeding your family. Period.

Parallel Tracking (Critical)

Time allocation:

- **2 hours/day:** Job search (applications, networking for full-time roles)
- **2-4 hours/day:** Income generation (freelancing, consulting, bridge work)

- **Rest:** Family, self-care, upskilling

DON'T spend all day job searching. Diminishing returns + no cash flow = disaster.

DO balance: Cash flow today + career building for tomorrow.

Case Studies

Suresh's consulting: Called 10 former clients from his 20-year career. Got 2 projects in the first month. Earned ₹80K. Took pressure off the job search.

Nisha's bridge: Started content writing on Upwork. Made ₹25-35K/month for 8 months while searching for the right full-time role. Never got desperate.

Arjun's pride trap: Refused any work he considered "beneath him." Ran out of money at month 5. Took a desperate job at 30% pay cut. Hates it to this day.

Action Steps

- List 20 people who might need your skills (former colleagues, clients, vendors, industry contacts)
- Create a simple consulting offer (one paragraph – what you offer, who needs it, how to reach you)
- Sign up for 3 freelance platforms relevant to your skill
- List assets you could sell if needed
- Week 1: Make 5 outreach calls or messages
- Week 2: Apply to 3 bridge income opportunities
- Target: Earn your first ₹1 by Week 2 (even ₹1,000 counts – momentum matters)

Key Takeaways

- Job search alone is financial suicide — you need bridge income
- Your 20-year career has immediately monetizable skills
- Every ₹10,000 earned = 1-2 weeks more runway = better decisions
- Pride is the enemy of survival; pragmatism is your friend

Part Two: Strategic Assessment (Days 31-60)

Chapter 4: The Seven Assets You Already Have

By the end of this chapter, you'll see you have MORE than you think — seven distinct assets to rebuild with.

Rekha, 46, felt completely worthless after her layoff. "I have nothing," she kept saying.

Then she did an honest audit: 22 years of marketing expertise. 500+ LinkedIn connections. ₹8 lakh in savings. A fully paid apartment. Excellent health. Supportive teenage kids. And something she'd never had before: time.

She had seven distinct assets. She'd just been too overwhelmed to see them.

The Seven Assets Framework

Most people count only one thing after a layoff: money. But you have seven distinct types of capital to rebuild with.

ASSET 1: Skills & Expertise

What you have:

- 15-25 years of domain knowledge that took decades to accumulate
- Technical skills (software, processes, systems your industry uses)
- Management experience (people, budgets, projects)

- Problem-solving ability specific to your industry

Audit questions:

- What can I teach? (Training, online courses, mentoring)
- What can I consult on? (Advisory, project-based work)
- What can I execute? (Freelance, contract work)

This is 20+ years of accumulated capital. It's yours, not your former employer's. They took the job, not the expertise.

ASSET 2: Network & Relationships

What you have:

- LinkedIn connections (100? 500? 2,000?)
- Industry relationships built over decades (vendors, partners, competitors)
- Professional associations and memberships
- College or university alumni network
- Former colleagues now in senior positions elsewhere

Audit questions:

- Who trusts my work? (These are your references and testimonials)
- Who would actually help me? (Real relationships vs. LinkedIn theater)
- Who needs what I offer? (Potential clients or employers)

One LinkedIn post about your availability can generate 5-10 leads. Your network is dormant capital – activate it.

ASSET 3: Financial Reserves

What you have:

- Savings and investments (even if smaller than you'd like)
- EPF balance (accessible after 60 days of unemployment)
- Gratuity (if you have 5+ years of service)
- Property equity (if applicable)
- Severance package

Do a net worth statement: Everything you own minus everything you owe. This is your runway. Strategic deployment of this asset determines how long you can play the game.

ASSET 4: Property & Physical Assets

What you have:

- Home (fully paid or with equity)
- Vehicle that could be monetized
- Equipment (laptop, phone, tools of your trade)
- Intellectual property (presentations, frameworks, tools you created)

Audit questions:

- What can generate income? (Rent a spare room, rent parking space, rent terrace)
- What can be sold if necessary? (Second vehicle, unused items)
- What enables income generation? (Your laptop is a consulting tool worth ₹50K/month in the right hands – yours)

ASSET 5: Health & Energy

What you have:

- Physical health (Can you work? For how many hours?)
- Mental resilience (Are you recovering from the initial shock?)
- Energy levels (Morning person? Night owl? Know your rhythm)
- Stamina (Can you work 50-hour weeks if needed?)

This is the foundation. Without health, nothing else works. Protect it: sleep, nutrition, exercise, stress management. If your health is compromised, address it first. Everything else depends on this.

ASSET 6: Knowledge & Learning Ability

What you have:

- Degrees and certifications (MBA, CA, engineering)
- Ability to learn new skills (your brain still works – probably better than at 25)
- Access to learning resources (internet, online courses, books)
- Pattern recognition from 20 years of experience (wisdom)

Audit questions:

- What can I learn in 3-6 months that's immediately marketable?
- What adjacent skills are in high demand in my industry?

- Can I add quick certifications? (PMP, Agile, specific software tools)

ASSET 7: Time & Flexibility

What you have that employed people don't:

- 40-50 hours per week suddenly available
- No commute time
- Flexibility to take consulting calls at any hour
- Ability to upskill during traditional "work hours"
- Geographic flexibility (Willing to relocate? Work remotely?)

Audit:

- How much time can you allocate to income generation? (20-30 hours/week)
- How much to job search? (10-15 hours/week)
- How much to upskilling? (5-10 hours/week)

This is a temporary asset. Once you're employed again, it's gone. Use it strategically now.

The Seven-Asset Scorecard

Take five minutes right now:

Rate each asset: **Strong (3) / Moderate (2) / Weak (1)**

Your three strongest assets = Lead with these. Your weakest asset = Either protect it or improve it.

Example: Strong network + strong expertise + weak financial reserves = Focus on consulting immediately. Leverage your strengths to build up your weakness.

Case Studies

Sanjay's audit: Once he listed all seven assets, he realized he wasn't starting from zero. He had more than enough to rebuild. The shift from despair to strategy happened in one afternoon.

Priya's hidden asset: She had a hobby blog with 5,000 followers she'd never monetized. One month after layoff, she offered consulting services to her readers. Made ₹8K the first month, ₹15K the next.

Mohan's network: One LinkedIn post: "After 18 years in supply chain, I'm available for consulting." Three consulting opportunities within a week.

Action Steps

- Complete a Seven Assets Audit (be thorough and honest)
- Rate each asset: Strong / Moderate / Weak
- Identify your 3 strongest assets (leverage these first)
- Identify your weakest asset (protect or improve)
- Create one specific action: "This week, I will leverage [strongest asset] by [specific action]"

Key Takeaways

- You're not starting from zero — you have seven distinct assets
- Your strongest assets show you the path forward
- The company decision to lay you off ≠ you have no value
- Most people only count money; you're now counting seven types of capital

Chapter 5: The Age Advantage (Reframing 40s-50s)

By the end of this chapter, you'll position your age as an advantage, not a liability.

Harish, 52, sat across from a 29-year-old interviewer. The question came: "Aren't you a bit... senior for this role?"

Harish fumbled. He apologized for his age. He tried to act younger. Rejected.

Next interview, different approach. Same question. New answer: "I've solved this exact problem at three different companies. Here's how, here's what I learned, here's what I can help you avoid."

Hired.

The Elephant in the Room

Age bias is real. Especially in tech, startups, and certain industries. Companies worry you're too expensive, not "culture fit," or technologically outdated.

Don't deny it. Strategize around it.

Victim mentality won't help you. Strategy will.

Why Age is Actually an Advantage (When Positioned Right)

Experience = Pattern Recognition

You've seen market cycles, crises, recoveries. You've seen strategies that worked and strategies that failed. You know the difference between what sounds good in a pitch deck and what actually works on Monday morning.

25-year-olds are brilliant. They're also learning from scratch. You already learned those lessons.

Network = Decades of Relationships

A 25-year-old has three years of professional relationships. You have 20+ years. Vendors who trust you. Clients who remember you. Industry contacts who take your call.

Depth beats breadth.

Stability = Lower Flight Risk

Employers' hidden fear: "Will they leave in 18 months?" With a 25-year-old, probably yes. With you? Likely more stable. You have family, roots, reasons to stay.

Frame it: "I'm here to build, not to browse."

Leadership = You've Done This Before

You've managed teams, budgets, crises. You can mentor junior employees, guide projects, lead initiatives. The 25-year-old needs mentoring. You provide it.

Frame it: "I hit the ground running and develop your junior team simultaneously."

Markets Where Age = Advantage

Don't fight uphill battles. Find your terrain.

Age is an advantage in:

1. **Consulting:** Clients want experience. Gray hair = credibility.
2. **Advisory roles:** Wisdom valued over speed.
3. **B2B sales:** Relationships matter more than energy.
4. **Niche expertise:** Deep knowledge beats broad generalist skills.
5. **Teaching/training:** You need credibility, which requires experience.
6. **Compliance/risk management:** Experience is crucial, not optional.

Age is a liability in:

- Hot startups looking for "culture fit"
- Cutting-edge tech companies that want 22-year-olds coding 16 hours/day

Choose your battles wisely.

The Positioning Strategy

DON'T:

- Apologize for your age ("I know I'm older, but...")
- Try to act young (it's fake and transparent)
- Accept below-market pay just "because age"
- Hide your experience or lie on your resume

DO:

- Lead with specific results ("Increased revenue 40% in 18 months")

- Emphasize outcomes, not years ("Launched 12 products, 9 succeeded")
- Show tech-savvy (Active LinkedIn, mention current tools: Slack, Asana, Zoom)
- Position as "senior expert," not "old employee"

The Script:

Interviewer: "You have a lot of experience..."

You: "Yes. I've solved this exact problem at [Company A] and [Company B]. Here's what I learned: [specific insight]. I can help you avoid [common expensive mistake] and accelerate to [desired outcome]. That's worth a lot more than saving ₹5 lakh on my salary."

Confidence. Specificity. Value.

Case Studies

Lakshmi, 48: Couldn't get hired in pharma companies (too expensive). Reframed as "20 years of pharma relationships and regulatory expertise." Became a sought-after consultant to smaller pharma firms. Makes ₹80K/month.

Vijay, 54: Spent 6 months applying for sales roles. Kept getting rejected. Pivoted to sales trainer for B2B companies. His age became his credibility. Now earns ₹2.5L/month.

Shruti, 50: Reframed her career as "Risk management expert who survived and led through the 2008 crash and 2020 pandemic." Got hired as CFO at a mid-sized company specifically because of that experience.

Action Steps

- Rewrite your LinkedIn summary using the positioning strategy above
- List 10 problems that ONLY experience can solve
- Identify 3 domains where your age is an advantage (not a liability)
- Practice the "I'm not too old, I'm experienced" conversation with a friend
- Apply to roles where age = asset (consulting, advisory, B2B)

Key Takeaways

- Age is a liability in some markets, an advantage in others — choose your battles
- Don't apologize or hide your experience — position it as valuable
- Results matter more than years: "I delivered X" beats "I have 20 years"
- The right employer values exactly what you bring

Part Three: Multiple Income Launch (Days 61-90)

Chapter 6: Your 90-Day Scorecard & Next Steps

By Day 90, you'll have stabilized financially and launched 1-2 income streams.

Return to Ramesh from the introduction.

Day 90 post-layoff:

- ₹45K/month from consulting (two clients)
- ₹15K/month teaching an online course
- Severance still intact due to strategic cost cutting
- Family united and supporting him
- Three job interviews scheduled

He's not back where he was. But he's stable, building, and the path forward is clear.

The 90-Day Assessment

Days 1-30: Stabilization

You should have:

✓ Completed emergency audit (Fortress Index calculated)
✓ Implemented cost cutting (₹15-30K/month saved)
✓ Generated immediate income (₹10-30K from assets or bridge work)
✓ Negotiated severance
✓ Communicated with family

Result: Runway extended, panic reduced, foundation stable.

Days 31-60: Assessment

You should have:

✓ Completed Seven Assets audit
✓ Identified your strongest assets
✓ Developed your age positioning strategy
✓ Started upskilling (if relevant)
✓ Activated your network

Result: Clarity on your path forward.

Days 61-90: Income Launch

You should have:

✓ Landed first consulting client OR freelance income (₹15-40K/month)
✓ Started second income stream OR received a job offer
✓ Established a sustainable routine (income generation + job search + family time)
✓ Stabilized financial position (not growing yet, but not depleting either)

Result: Crisis has transformed into stability.

Measuring Success (Realistic Expectations)
If you started in GREEN zone (6+ months runway):

- **Target:** Strategic job search + 1 income stream
- **Success:** Job offer OR ₹30K+/month consulting income
- **Timeline:** 90 days is realistic

If you started in YELLOW zone (3-6 months runway):

- **Target:** Immediate income + aggressive job search
- **Success:** ₹25-40K/month bridge income + active job pipeline (interviews scheduled)
- **Timeline:** 60-90 days

If you started in RED zone (<3 months runway):

- **Target:** ANY income immediately
- **Success:** ₹20-30K/month within 30 days from any ethical source
- **Timeline:** 30 days – you had no luxury of time

What Happens After Day 90

Scenario 1: You got a job

Congratulations. But don't stop here.

Keep your side income stream active. Never depend entirely on one job again. Build a 12-month emergency fund. The world just taught you a valuable lesson – learn it.

Scenario 2: No job yet, but income streams are working

Continue building your streams. ₹40K/month can become ₹70K/month over the next 6 months. Consider whether a portfolio career (multiple income sources, no single employer) might actually be better than traditional employment.

Many people discover they prefer this model.

Scenario 3: Still struggling

Be honest: What's blocking you?

- **Skills outdated?** Address it through focused upskilling.
- **Network weak?** Rebuild it systematically – one coffee chat per week.
- **Health issues?** Address these first. Nothing works without health.

Seek support: Outplacement services, career counselors, community resources.

Don't give up. The average job search for 40+ professionals is 6-8 months. You're not failing – the timeline is just realistic.

Case Studies Revisited (Day 90)

Ramesh: ₹60K/month combined income (consulting + teaching), actively negotiating a full-time offer with leverage (not desperation)

Sunita: ₹35K/month freelance income, 4 job interviews in pipeline, runway stable and extended

Amit (the cautionary tale): Month 6, still only job searching with no bridge income, savings almost gone, now taking the first desperate offer available

Action Steps

- Complete your 90-day self-assessment
- Measure: Runway then vs. now (Did you extend it? Maintain it?)
- Measure: Income streams (Did you go from 0 to 1-2?)

- Set your next 90-day goals:
  - If employed: Build 12-month emergency fund + keep side income active
  - If not yet employed: Scale income to ₹60-80K/month + continue strategic job search
- Schedule a 6-month review to assess long-term direction

Key Takeaways

- 90 days = stabilization, not full recovery (that takes 6-12 months)
- Success is runway extended + income launched, not "back to old job"
- This is Phase 1; Phase 2 is thriving, not just surviving

You're Not Done, You're Rebuilt

You survived the crisis (Days 1-30).

You assessed your assets honestly (Days 31-60).

You launched new income (Days 61-90).

You're not back where you were. That job is gone, and honestly, that's probably a good thing. That model – one job, total dependence, complete vulnerability – was fragile.

You're now building something different: resilience, diversification, multiple income streams. You're building antifragility.

The old model: One job, one income source, one point of total failure.

The new model: Multiple income streams, no single point of failure, resilience built into the structure.

Yes, you were laid off. Yes, it was painful. Yes, it disrupted everything.

But you're not the same person you were 90 days ago. You're more resilient. You're more resourceful. You're more realistic about how the modern economy actually works.

The ground shifted. You didn't fall. You rebuilt.

What's next?

If you're employed again: Build that 12-month emergency fund. Keep your side income active. Never again depend entirely on one employer's decision about your worth.

If you're still building: Keep going. Scale your income streams. Month 6 looks different than Month 3. You're not failing – you're building something that actually lasts.

This isn't the end. It's the foundation.

You've got this.

About this Book Series

This is Book 1 in the *Modern Career Security* series, applying timeless strategic principles to today's volatile job market. Book 2: *Never Depend on One Job Again* covers building multiple income streams to ₹80K-1.5L/month.

www.ingramcontent.com/pod-product-compliance
Lightning Source LLC
Chambersburg PA
CBHW011803160726
48282CB00035B/1246

* 9 7 8 9 3 4 7 3 6 5 2 4 9 *